MznLnx

Missing Links Exam Preps

Exam Prep for

Practical Business Math Procedures

Slater, 7th Edition

The MznLnx Exam Prep is your link from the texbook and lecture to your exams.
The MznLnx Exam Preps are unauthorized and comprehensive reviews of your textbooks.

All material provided by MznLnx and Rico Publications (c) 2010
Textbook publishers and textbook authors do not particpate in or contribute to these reviews.

MznLnx

Rico Publications

Exam Prep for Practical Business Math Procedures
7th Edition
Slater

Publisher: Raymond Houge
Assistant Editor: Michael Rouger
Text and Cover Designer: Lisa Buckner
Marketing Manager: Sara Swagger
Project Manager, Editorial Production: Jerry Emerson
Art Director: Vernon Lowerui

Product Manager: Dave Mason
Editorial Assitant: Rachel Guzmanji
Pedagogy: Debra Long
Cover Image: Jim Reed/Getty Images
Text and Cover Printer: City Printing, Inc.
Compositor: Media Mix, Inc.

(c) 2010 Rico Publications
ALL RIGHTS RESERVED. No part of this work covered by the copyright may be reproduced or used in any form or by an means--graphic, electronic, or mechanical, including photocopying, recording, taping, Web distribution, information storage, and retrieval systems, or in any other manner--without the written permission of the publisher.

For more information about our products, contact us at:
Dave.Mason@RicoPublications.com

For permission to use material from this text or product, submit a request online to:
Dave.Mason@RicoPublications.com

Printed in the United States
ISBN:

Contents

CHAPTER 1
Whole Numbers; How to Dissect and Solve Word Problems — 1

CHAPTER 2
Fractions — 6

CHAPTER 3
Decimals — 9

CHAPTER 4
Banking — 11

CHAPTER 5
Solving for the Unknown: A How-to Approach — 13

CHAPTER 6
Percents and Their Applications — 14

CHAPTER 7
Discounts: Trade and Cash — 16

CHAPTER 8
Markups and Markdowns; Insight into Perishables — 20

CHAPTER 9
Payroll — 22

CHAPTER 10
Simple Interest — 24

CHAPTER 11
Promissory Notes, Simple Discount Notes, and the Discount Process — 26

CHAPTER 12
Compound Interest and Present Value — 29

CHAPTER 13
Annuities and Sinking Funds — 31

CHAPTER 14
Installment Buying, Rule of 78, and Revolving Charge Credit Cards — 32

CHAPTER 15
The Cost of Home Ownership — 35

CHAPTER 16
How to Read, Analyze, and Interpret Financial Reports — 38

CHAPTER 17
Depreciation — 43

CHAPTER 18
Inventory and Overhead — 45

CHAPTER 19
Sales, Excise, and Property Taxes — 47

CHAPTER 20
Life, Fire, and Auto Insurance — 48

Contents (Cont.)

CHAPTER 21
Stocks, Bonds, and Mutual Funds   52
CHAPTER 22
Business Statistics   54
ANSWER KEY   60

TO THE STUDENT

COMPREHENSIVE

The *MznLnx* Exam Prep series is designed to help you pass your exams. Editors at MznLnx review your textbooks and then prepare these practice exams to help you master the textbook material. Unlike study guides, workbooks, and practice tests provided by the texbook publisher and textbook authors, *MznLnx* gives you **all** of the material in each chapter in exam form, not just samples, so you can be sure to nail your exam.

MECHANICAL

The MznLnx Exam Prep series creates exams that will help you learn the subject matter as well as test you on your understanding. Each question is designed to help you master the concept. Just working through the exams, you gain an understanding of the subject--its a simple mechanical process that produces success.

INTEGRATED STUDY GUIDE AND REVIEW

MznLnx is not just a set of exams designed to test you, its also a comprehensive review of the subject content. Each exam question is also a review of the concept, making sure that you will get the answer correct without having to go to other sources of material. You learn as you go! Its the easiest way to pass an exam.

HUMOR

Studying can be tedious and dry. MznLnx's instructional design includes moderate humor within the exam questions on occassion, to break the tedium and revitalize the brain

Chapter 1. Whole Numbers; How to Dissect and Solve Word Problems

1. In a positional numeral system, the decimal separator is a symbol used to mark the boundary between the integral and the fractional parts of a decimal numeral. When used in context of Arabic numerals, terms implying the symbol used are _____ and decimal comma.

   The decimal separator is mathematically a radix point.

   a. Hexadecimal
   b. Tetradecimal
   c. Decimal point
   d. Fibonacci coding

2. The _____ is a positional numeral system; it has positions for units, tens, hundreds, etc. The position of each digit conveys the multiplier (a power of ten) to be used with that digit—each position has a value ten times that of the position to its right.
   a. Composite
   b. Cleaver
   c. Decimal system
   d. Free

3. In mathematics, the _____ is a term used to describe the number of times one must apply a given operation to an integer before reaching a fixed point.

   Usually, this refers to the additive or multiplicative persistence of an integer, which is how often one has to replace the number by the sum or product of its digits until one reaches a single digit. Because the numbers are broken down into their digits, the additive or multiplicative persistence depends on the radix.

   a. Persistence of a number
   b. Coprime
   c. Lychrel number
   d. Linear congruence theorem

4. _____ is a numeral system in which each position is related to the next by a constant multiplier, a common ratio, called the base or radix of that numeral system.
   a. NegaFibonacci coding
   b. Cyrillic numerals
   c. Negative base
   d. Place value

Chapter 1. Whole Numbers; How to Dissect and Solve Word Problems

5. In mathematics, a _____ can mean either an element of the set {1, 2, 3, ...} (i.e the positive integers) or an element of the set {0, 1, 2, 3, ...} (i.e. the non-negative integers).
   a. Bounded
   b. FISH
   c. Whole number
   d. Degrees of freedom

6. The quantity that is deducted from the minuend in subtraction is the _____.
   a. Trailing zeros
   b. Lowest common denominator
   c. The number 0 is even.
   d. Subtrahend

7. A _____ is a deliberate process for transforming one or more inputs into one or more results, with variable change.

The term is used in a variety of senses, from the very definite arithmetical using an algorithm to the vague heuristics of calculating a strategy in a competition or calculating the chance of a successful relationship between two people.

Multiplying 7 by 8 is a simple algorithmic _____.

   a. Mathematical object
   b. Mathematical maturity
   c. Mathematics Subject Classification
   d. Calculation

8. _____ involves reducing the number of significant digits in a number. The result of _____ is a 'shorter' number having fewer non-zero digits yet similar in magnitude. The result is less precise but easier to use.
   a. Rounding
   b. Shabakh
   c. Sudan function
   d. Hyper operator

9. The traditional names for the parts of the formula c − b = a, are _____ (c) − subtrahend (b) = difference (a). The words _____ and subtrahend are uncommon in modern usage. Instead we say that c and −b are terms, and treat subtraction as addition of the opposite. The answer is still called the difference.

a. Lowest common denominator
b. Minuend
c. Multiplication
d. Plus and minus signs

10. In mathematics, especially in the area of abstract algebra known as combinatorial group theory, the _____ for a recursively presented group G is the algorithmic problem of deciding whether two words represent the same element. Although it is common to speak of the _____ for the group G strictly speaking it is a presentation of the group that does or does not have solvable _____. Given two finite presentations P and Q of a group G, P has solvable _____ if and only if Q does.
a. Torsion
b. Prime ideal theorem
c. Computational mathematics
d. Word problem

11. An _____ is a number which is involved in addition. A number being added is considered to be an _____.
a. A chemical equation
b. A Mathematical Theory of Communication
c. Addend
d. A posteriori

12. _____ is the mathematical operation of scaling one number by another. It is one of the four basic operations in elementary arithmetic.

_____ is defined for whole numbers in terms of repeated addition; for example, 4 multiplied by 3 can be calculated by adding 3 copies of 4 together:

$$4 + 4 + 4 = 12.$$

_____ of rational numbers and real numbers is defined by systematic generalization of this basic idea.

a. Highest common factor
b. The number 0 is even.
c. Least common multiple
d. Multiplication

Chapter 1. Whole Numbers; How to Dissect and Solve Word Problems

13. In Fourier analysis, a _____ is a kind of linear operator, or transformation of functions. These operators multiply the Fourier coefficients of a function by a specified function, hence the name. Among the multipliers one can count some simple operators, such as translations and differentiation, but also some more complicated ones such as the convolutions, Hilbert transform, and others.
    a. Poisson summation formula
    b. Reality condition
    c. Fourier multiplier
    d. Modulated complex lapped transform

14. In mathematics, for a sequence of numbers $a_1, a_2, a_3, \ldots$ the infinite product

$$\prod_{n=1}^{\infty} a_n = a_1 \, a_2 \, a_3 \cdots$$

is defined to be the limit of the _____ $a_1 a_2 \ldots a_n$ as n increases without bound. The product is said to converge when the limit exists and is not zero.

   a. Bounded variation
   b. Semi-continuity
   c. Quasiconvex function
   d. Partial products

15. A _____ is a deliberate plan of action to guide decisions and achieve rational outcom. The term may apply to government, private sector organizations and groups, and individuals. Presidential executive orders, corporate privacy policies, and parliamentary rules of order are all examples of _____.
    a. 1-center problem
    b. Policy
    c. 120-cell
    d. 2-3 heap

16. _____s are payments made by a corporation to its shareholder members. When a corporation earns a profit or surplus, that money can be put to two uses: it can either be re-invested in the business, or it can be paid to the shareholders as a _____. Many corporations retain a portion of their earnings and pay the remainder as a _____.
    a. 120-cell
    b. 1-center problem
    c. GNU Privacy Guard
    d. Dividend

17. In mathematics, a _____ of an integer n is an integer which evenly divides n without leaving a remainder.

For example, 7 is a _____ of 42 because 42/7 = 6. We also say 42 is divisible by 7 or 42 is a multiple of 7 or 7 divides 42 or 7 is a factor of 42 and we usually write 7 | 42.

   a. 2-3 heap
   b. Divisor
   c. 1-center problem
   d. 120-cell

18. In mathematics, a _____ is the end result of a division problem. It can also be expressed as the number of times the divisor divides into the dividend.
   a. Notation
   b. Marginal cost
   c. Limiting
   d. Quotient

Chapter 2. Fractions

1. A vulgar fraction (or common fraction) is a rational number written as one integer (the numerator) divided by a non-zero integer (the denominator).

A vulgar fraction is said to be a _____ if the absolute value of the numerator is less than the absolute value of the denominator--that is, if the absolute value of the entire fraction is less than 1.

   a. Proper fraction
   b. 1-center problem
   c. Farey sequence
   d. 120-cell

2. In mathematics, the _____, sometimes known as the greatest common factor or highest common factor, of two non-zero integers, is the largest positive integer that divides both numbers without remainder.

This notion can be extended to polynomials, see _____ of two polynomials.

The _____ of a and b is written as gc, or sometimes simply as.

   a. Multiplication
   b. Minuend
   c. Highest common factor
   d. Greatest common divisor

3. In mathematics, a _____ of an integer n is an integer which evenly divides n without leaving a remainder.

For example, 7 is a _____ of 42 because 42/7 = 6. We also say 42 is divisible by 7 or 42 is a multiple of 7 or 7 divides 42 or 7 is a factor of 42 and we usually write 7 | 42.

   a. 2-3 heap
   b. Divisor
   c. 1-center problem
   d. 120-cell

4. In the study of metric spaces in mathematics, there are various notions of two metrics on the same underlying space being 'the same', or _____.

In the following, M will denote a non-empty set and d_1 and d_2 will denote two metrics on M.

The two metrics d_1 and d_2 are said to be topologically _____ if they generate the same topology on M.

Chapter 2. Fractions

a. A Mathematical Theory of Communication
b. A chemical equation
c. A posteriori
d. Equivalent

5. In mathematics, the multiplicative inverse of a number x, denoted 1/x or x $^{-1}$, is the number which, when multiplied by x, yields 1. The multiplicative inverse of x is also called the _____ of x.

a. 1-center problem
b. 2-3 heap
c. Reciprocal
d. 120-cell

6. In mathematics, the _____ or least common denominator is the least common multiple of the denominators of a set of vulgar fractions. It is the smallest positive integer that is a multiple of the denominators. For instance, the _____ of

$$\left\{\frac{5}{12}, \frac{11}{18}\right\}$$

is 36 because the least common multiple of 12 and 18 is 36.

a. Highest common factor
b. The number 0 is even.
c. Lowest common denominator
d. Subtrahend

7. In mathematics, a _____ is a natural number which has exactly two distinct natural number divisors: 1 and itself. An infinitude of _____s exists, as demonstrated by Euclid around 300 BC. The first twenty-five _____s are:

2, 3, 5, 7, 11, 13, 17, 19, 23, 29, 31, 37, 41, 43, 47, 53, 59, 61, 67, 71, 73, 79, 83, 89, 97.

a. Pronic number
b. Highly composite number
c. Prime number
d. Perrin number

8. A calculation is a deliberate process for transforming one or more inputs into one or more results, with variable change.

8   *Chapter 2. Fractions*

The term is used in a variety of senses, from the very definite arithmetical using an algorithm to the vague heuristics of _____ a strategy in a competition or _____ the chance of a successful relationship between two people.

Multiplying 7 by 8 is a simple algorithmic calculation.

   a. Calculating
   b. Calculation
   c. Mathematical maturity
   d. Mathematics Subject Classification

9. _____ is the mathematical operation of scaling one number by another. It is one of the four basic operations in elementary arithmetic.

_____ is defined for whole numbers in terms of repeated addition; for example, 4 multiplied by 3 can be calculated by adding 3 copies of 4 together:

$$4 + 4 + 4 = 12.$$

_____ of rational numbers and real numbers is defined by systematic generalization of this basic idea.

   a. Multiplication
   b. Highest common factor
   c. The number 0 is even.
   d. Least common multiple

10. A _____ is a deliberate plan of action to guide decisions and achieve rational outcom. The term may apply to government, private sector organizations and groups, and individuals. Presidential executive orders, corporate privacy policies, and parliamentary rules of order are all examples of _____.

   a. 1-center problem
   b. 2-3 heap
   c. 120-cell
   d. Policy

Chapter 4. Banking

1. In mathematics, the _____ of an oriented manifold M is defined when M has dimension d divisible by four. In that case, when M is connected and orientable, cup product gives rise to a quadratic form Q on the 'middle' real cohomology group

   H^{2n}

where

   d = 4n.

The basic identity for the cup product

$$\alpha^p \smile \beta^q = (-1)^{pq}(\beta^q \smile \alpha^p)$$

shows that with p = q = 2n the product is commutative.

   a. Branched surface
   b. Mapping class group
   c. Seifert surface
   d. Signature

2. A _____ is a type of affix attached to a stem which modifies the meaning of that stem.

The word '_____' is itself made up of the stem fix, and the _____ pre-, both of which are derived from Latin roots.

   - English _____es
   - _____es and suffixes in Hebrew

   a. 120-cell
   b. 1-center problem
   c. 2-3 heap
   d. Prefix

3. In mathematics, the _____ in group theory is a group homomorphism defined given a finite group G and a subgroup H, which goes from the abelianization of G to that of H.

To define the _____, take coset representatives for the left cosets of H in G, say

$$g_1, \ldots, g_k.$$

Given g in G, it is always possible to write

$$g \cdot g_i = g_j \cdot h_i(g)$$

with some index j and some h_i

$$g \cdot g_i H$$

is.

a. Bounded
b. Transfer
c. Class
d. Critical point

Chapter 5. Solving for the Unknown: A How-to Approach

1. In mathematics and in the sciences, a _____ (plural: _____e, formulæ or _____s) is a concise way of expressing information symbolically (as in a mathematical or chemical _____), or a general relationship between quantities. One of many famous _____e is Albert Einstein's $E = mc^2$ (see special relativity

In mathematics, a _____ is a key to solve an equation with variables. For example, the problem of determining the volume of a sphere is one that requires a significant amount of integral calculus to solve.

   a. 1-center problem
   b. Formula
   c. 2-3 heap
   d. 120-cell

2. In mathematics, especially in the area of abstract algebra known as combinatorial group theory, the _____ for a recursively presented group G is the algorithmic problem of deciding whether two words represent the same element. Although it is common to speak of the _____ for the group G strictly speaking it is a presentation of the group that does or does not have solvable _____. Given two finite presentations P and Q of a group G, P has solvable _____ if and only if Q does.
   a. Computational mathematics
   b. Torsion
   c. Prime ideal theorem
   d. Word problem

Chapter 6. Percents and Their Applications

1. In mathematics, _____ and undefined are used to explain whether or not expressions have meaningful, sensible, and unambiguous values. Not all branches of mathematics come to the same conclusion.

The following expressions are undefined in all contexts, but remarks in the analysis section may apply.

  a. LHS
  b. Plugging in
  c. Toy model
  d. Defined

2. A _____ is the result of applying a function to a set of data.

More formally, statistical theory defines a _____ as a function of a sample where the function itself is independent of the sample's distribution: the term is used both for the function and for the value of the function on a given sample.

A _____ is distinct from an unknown statistical parameter, which is not computable from a sample.

  a. Statistic
  b. Spatial dependence
  c. Parameter space
  d. Loss function

3. _____ is a mathematical science pertaining to the collection, analysis, interpretation or explanation, and presentation of data. It also provides tools for prediction and forecasting based on data. It is applicable to a wide variety of academic disciplines, from the natural and social sciences to the humanities, government and business.
  a. Statistics
  b. Percentile rank
  c. Regression toward the mean
  d. Probability distribution

4. _____ involves reducing the number of significant digits in a number. The result of _____ is a 'shorter' number having fewer non-zero digits yet similar in magnitude. The result is less precise but easier to use.
  a. Shabakh
  b. Sudan function
  c. Rounding
  d. Hyper operator

Chapter 6. Percents and Their Applications

5. In mathematics and computer science, _____ (also base-16, hexa or base, of 16. It uses sixteen distinct symbols, most often the symbols 0-9 to represent values zero to nine, and A, B, C, D, E, F (or a through f) to represent values ten to fifteen.

Its primary use is as a human friendly representation of binary coded values, so it is often used in digital electronics and computer engineering.

   a. Tetradecimal
   b. Radix
   c. Hexadecimal
   d. Factoradic

6. In mathematics, a _____ is a way of expressing a number as a fraction of 100. It is often denoted using the percent sign, '%'. For example, 45% is equal to 45 / 100, or 0.45.
   a. Lowest common denominator
   b. Percentage
   c. Subtrahend
   d. Least common multiple

Chapter 7. Discounts: Trade and Cash

1. _____ involves reducing the number of significant digits in a number. The result of _____ is a 'shorter' number having fewer non-zero digits yet similar in magnitude. The result is less precise but easier to use.
    a. Sudan function
    b. Rounding
    c. Shabakh
    d. Hyper operator

2. The quantity that is deducted from the minuend in subtraction is the _____.
    a. Lowest common denominator
    b. Subtrahend
    c. Trailing zeros
    d. The number 0 is even.

3. In mathematics, a _____ can mean either an element of the set {1, 2, 3, ...} (i.e the positive integers) or an element of the set {0, 1, 2, 3, ...} (i.e. the non-negative integers).
    a. FISH
    b. Degrees of freedom
    c. Whole number
    d. Bounded

4. In discrete mathematics and predominantly in set theory, a _____ is a concept used in comparisons of sets to refer to the unique values of one set in relation to another. The terms 'absolute' and 'relative' _____ refer to more specific applications of the concept, with universal _____s referring to elements unique to the universal set and the latter referring to the unique elements of one set in relation to another. In this image, the universal set is represented by the border of the image, and the set A as a disc.
    a. Derivative algebra
    b. Kernel
    c. Huge
    d. Complement

5. In finance, the Acid-test or _____ or liquid ratio measures the ability of a company to use its near cash or quick assets to immediately extinguish or retire its current liabilities. Quick assets include those current assets that presumably can be quickly converted to cash at close to their book values.

$$\text{Quick (Acid Test) Ratio} = \frac{\text{Cash} + \text{Marketable Securities} + \text{Accounts Receivables}}{\text{Current Liabilities}}$$

Generally, the acid test ratio should be 1:1 or better, however this varies widely by industry.

a. 1-center problem
b. 120-cell
c. Quick ratio
d. 2-3 heap

6. In mathematics, a _____ is often represented as the sum of a sequence of terms. That is, a _____ is represented as a list of numbers with addition operations between them, for example this arithmetic sequence:

   $1 + 2 + 3 + 4 + 5 + ... + 99 + 100$

In most cases of interest the terms of the sequence are produced according to a certain rule, such as by a formula, by an algorithm, by a sequence of measurements, or even by a random number generator.

a. Concavity
b. Blind
c. Series
d. Contact

7. In the study of metric spaces in mathematics, there are various notions of two metrics on the same underlying space being 'the same', or _____.

In the following, M will denote a non-empty set and d_1 and d_2 will denote two metrics on M.

The two metrics d_1 and d_2 are said to be topologically _____ if they generate the same topology on M.

a. A chemical equation
b. A Mathematical Theory of Communication
c. A posteriori
d. Equivalent

8. _____ is the concept of adding accumulated interest back to the principal, so that interest is earned on interest from that moment on. The act of declaring interest to be principal is called compounding. A loan, for example, may have its interest compounded every month: in this case, a loan with $100 principal and 1% interest per month would have a balance of $101 at the end of the first month.

Chapter 7. Discounts: Trade and Cash

   a. Net interest margin
   b. Compound interest
   c. Net interest margin securities
   d. Retained interest

9. _____ is a fee, paid on borrowed capital. Assets lent include money, shares, consumer goods through hire purchase, major assets such as aircraft, and even entire factories in finance lease arrangements. The _____ is calculated upon the value of the assets in the same manner as upon money.
   a. Interest sensitivity gap
   b. A Mathematical Theory of Communication
   c. Interest expense
   d. Interest

10. In mathematics, a _____ is a number that can be expressed as an integral of an algebraic function over an algebraic domain. Kontsevich and Zagier define a _____ as a complex number whose real and imaginary parts are values of absolutely convergent integrals of rational functions with rational coefficients, over domains in given by polynomial inequalities with rational coefficients.
   a. Boussinesq approximation
   b. Period
   c. Closeness
   d. Disk

11. A calculation is a deliberate process for transforming one or more inputs into one or more results, with variable change.

The term is used in a variety of senses, from the very definite arithmetical using an algorithm to the vague heuristics of _____ a strategy in a competition or _____ the chance of a successful relationship between two people.

Multiplying 7 by 8 is a simple algorithmic calculation.

   a. Calculating
   b. Mathematical maturity
   c. Calculation
   d. Mathematics Subject Classification

12. _____ is a 2000 epic film directed by Ridley Scott and starring Russell Crowe, Joaquin Phoenix, Connie Nielsen, Oliver Reed, Djimon Hounsou, Derek Jacobi and Richard Harris. Crowe portrays General Maximus Decimus Meridius, friend of Emperor Marcus Aurelius who is betrayed and murdered by his ambitious son, Commodus (Phoenix.) Captured and enslaved along the outer fringes of the Roman empire, Maximus rises through the ranks of the gladiatorial arena to avenge the murder of his family and his Emperor.
   a. Agnes Meyer Driscoll
   b. Gladiator
   c. Adi Shamir
   d. Abraham Sinkov

Chapter 8. Markups and Markdowns; Insight into Perishables

1. In economics, business, retail, and accounting, a _____ is the value of money that has been used up to produce something, and hence is not available for use anymore. In business, the _____ may be one of acquisition, in which case the amount of money expended to acquire it is counted as _____. In this case, money is the input that is gone in order to acquire the thing.
   a. 120-cell
   b. Cost
   c. 2-3 heap
   d. 1-center problem

2. In accounting, _____ or sales profit is the difference between revenue and the cost of making a product or providing a service, before deducting overhead, payroll, taxation, and interest payments. Note that this is different than operating profit.

Net sales are calculated:

   Net sales = Sales - Sales returns and allowances

_____ is found by deducting the cost of goods sold:

   _____ = Net sales - Cost of goods sold

_____ should not be confused with net income:

   Net income = _____ - Total operating expenses

Cost of goods sold is calculated differently for merchandising business than for a manufacturer.

   a. 1-center problem
   b. Gross profit
   c. 2-3 heap
   d. 120-cell

3. A vulgar fraction (or common fraction) is a rational number written as one integer (the numerator) divided by a non-zero integer (the denominator).

A vulgar fraction is said to be a _____ if the absolute value of the numerator is less than the absolute value of the denominator--that is, if the absolute value of the entire fraction is less than 1.

Chapter 8. Markups and Markdowns; Insight into Perishables

a. 120-cell
b. Proper fraction
c. Farey sequence
d. 1-center problem

4. In the study of metric spaces in mathematics, there are various notions of two metrics on the same underlying space being 'the same', or _____.

In the following, M will denote a non-empty set and d_1 and d_2 will denote two metrics on M.

The two metrics d_1 and d_2 are said to be topologically _____ if they generate the same topology on M.

a. A Mathematical Theory of Communication
b. A posteriori
c. A chemical equation
d. Equivalent

5. _____ is a lightweight markup language, originally created by John Gruber and Aaron Swartz to help maximum readability and 'publishability' of both its input and output forms. The language takes many cues from existing conventions for marking up plain text in email. _____ converts its marked-up text input to valid, well-formed XHTML and replaces left-pointing angle brackets ('<') and ampersands with their corresponding character entity references.

a. Markdown
b. 120-cell
c. 2-3 heap
d. 1-center problem

Chapter 9. Payroll

1. In the study of metric spaces in mathematics, there are various notions of two metrics on the same underlying space being 'the same', or _____.

In the following, M will denote a non-empty set and d_1 and d_2 will denote two metrics on M.

The two metrics d_1 and d_2 are said to be topologically _____ if they generate the same topology on M.

   a. A chemical equation
   b. Equivalent
   c. A Mathematical Theory of Communication
   d. A posteriori

2. Suppose that φ : M → N is a smooth map between smooth manifolds; then the _____ of φ at a point x is, in some sense, the best linear approximation of φ near x. It can be viewed as generalization of the total derivative of ordinary calculus. Explicitly, it is a linear map from the tangent space of M at x to the tangent space of N at φ
   a. Grill
   b. Boundary
   c. Concurrent
   d. Differential

3. In abstract algebra, a module S over a ring R is called _____ or irreducible if it is not the zero module 0 and if its only submodules are 0 and S. Understanding the _____ modules over a ring is usually helpful because these modules form the 'building blocks' of all other modules in a certain sense.

Abelian groups are the same as Z-modules.

   a. Basis
   b. Derivation
   c. Harmonic series
   d. Simple

4. A _____ is a party that mediates between a buyer and a seller. A _____ who also acts as a seller or as a buyer becomes a principal party to the deal. Distinguish agent: one who acts on behalf of a principal.
   a. 1-center problem
   b. 120-cell
   c. Broker
   d. 2-3 heap

Chapter 9. Payroll

5.

A _____ is an official document affirming some fact. For example, a birth _____ or death _____ testifies to basic facts regarding a person's birth or death. A _____ may also certify that a person has received specific education or has passed a test, and is considered below the standard of an academic degree.

   a. Certificate
   b. 1-center problem
   c. 2-3 heap
   d. 120-cell

6. In mathematics, a _____ is a way of expressing a number as a fraction of 100. It is often denoted using the percent sign, '%'. For example, 45% is equal to 45 / 100, or 0.45.
   a. Lowest common denominator
   b. Least common multiple
   c. Subtrahend
   d. Percentage

7. _____ is a fee, paid on borrowed capital. Assets lent include money, shares, consumer goods through hire purchase, major assets such as aircraft, and even entire factories in finance lease arrangements. The _____ is calculated upon the value of the assets in the same manner as upon money.
   a. Interest sensitivity gap
   b. Interest
   c. Interest expense
   d. A Mathematical Theory of Communication

Chapter 10. Simple Interest

1. _____ is a fee, paid on borrowed capital. Assets lent include money, shares, consumer goods through hire purchase, major assets such as aircraft, and even entire factories in finance lease arrangements. The _____ is calculated upon the value of the assets in the same manner as upon money.
   a. A Mathematical Theory of Communication
   b. Interest sensitivity gap
   c. Interest expense
   d. Interest

2. _____ is a lightweight markup language, originally created by John Gruber and Aaron Swartz to help maximum readability and 'publishability' of both its input and output forms. The language takes many cues from existing conventions for marking up plain text in email. _____ converts its marked-up text input to valid, well-formed XHTML and replaces left-pointing angle brackets ('<') and ampersands with their corresponding character entity references.
   a. 120-cell
   b. 2-3 heap
   c. 1-center problem
   d. Markdown

3. In abstract algebra, a module S over a ring R is called _____ or irreducible if it is not the zero module 0 and if its only submodules are 0 and S. Understanding the _____ modules over a ring is usually helpful because these modules form the 'building blocks' of all other modules in a certain sense.

Abelian groups are the same as Z-modules.

   a. Basis
   b. Derivation
   c. Harmonic series
   d. Simple

4. In computational complexity theory, an algorithm is said to take _____ if the asymptotic upper bound for the time it requires is proportional to the size of the input, which is usually denoted n.

Informally spoken, the running time increases linearly with the size of the input. For example, a procedure that adds up all elements of a list requires time proportional to the length of the list.

   a. Time-constructible function
   b. Truth table reduction
   c. Constructible function
   d. Linear time

5. In mathematics, a _____ is an algebraic structure consisting of a set together with an operation that combines any two of its elements to form a third element. To qualify as a _____, the set and operation must satisfy a few conditions called _____ axioms, namely associativity, identity and invertibility. While these are familiar from many mathematical structures, such as number systems--for example, the integers endowed with the addition operation form a _____--the formulation of the axioms is detached from the concrete nature of the _____ and its operation.

a. Characteristic function
b. Derivative algebra
c. Coherence
d. Group

Chapter 11. Promissory Notes, Simple Discount Notes, and the Discount Process

1. _____ is a lightweight markup language, originally created by John Gruber and Aaron Swartz to help maximum readability and 'publishability' of both its input and output forms. The language takes many cues from existing conventions for marking up plain text in email. _____ converts its marked-up text input to valid, well-formed XHTML and replaces left-pointing angle brackets ('<') and ampersands with their corresponding character entity references.
   a. 1-center problem
   b. 2-3 heap
   c. 120-cell
   d. Markdown

2. The term _____ refers to the central sense organ complex, for those animals that have one, normally on the ventral surface of the head and can depending on the definition in the human case, include the hair, forehead, eyebrow, eyes, nose, ears, cheeks, mouth, lips, philtrum, teeth, skin, and chin. The _____ has uses of expression, appearance, and identity amongst others.It also has different senses like smelling, tasting, hearing, and seeing.

   Caricatures often exaggerate facial features to make a _____ more easily recognized in association with a pronounced portion of the _____ of the individual in question--for example, a caricature of Osama bin Laden might focus on his facial hair and nose; a caricature of George W. Bush might enlarge his ears to the size of an elephant¢s; a caricature of Jay Leno may pronounce his head and chin; and a caricature of Mick Jagger might enlarge his lips.

   a. 2-3 heap
   b. 120-cell
   c. 1-center problem
   d. Face

3. _____ is an acronym which stands for last in, first out. In computer science and queueing theory this refers to the way items stored in some types of data structures are processed. By definition, in a _____ structured linear list, elements can be added or taken off from only one end, called the 'top'.
   a. 1-center problem
   b. LIFO
   c. 2-3 heap
   d. 120-cell

4. In abstract algebra, a module S over a ring R is called _____ or irreducible if it is not the zero module 0 and if its only submodules are 0 and S. Understanding the _____ modules over a ring is usually helpful because these modules form the 'building blocks' of all other modules in a certain sense.

   Abelian groups are the same as Z-modules.

Chapter 11. Promissory Notes, Simple Discount Notes, and the Discount Process

a. Harmonic series
b. Derivation
c. Basis
d. Simple

5. In the study of metric spaces in mathematics, there are various notions of two metrics on the same underlying space being 'the same', or _____.

In the following, M will denote a non-empty set and d_1 and d_2 will denote two metrics on M.

The two metrics d_1 and d_2 are said to be topologically _____ if they generate the same topology on M.

a. A chemical equation
b. A Mathematical Theory of Communication
c. A posteriori
d. Equivalent

6. A _____ is a deliberate plan of action to guide decisions and achieve rational outcom. The term may apply to government, private sector organizations and groups, and individuals. Presidential executive orders, corporate privacy policies, and parliamentary rules of order are all examples of _____.
a. 1-center problem
b. 2-3 heap
c. Policy
d. 120-cell

7. _____ is a fee, paid on borrowed capital. Assets lent include money, shares, consumer goods through hire purchase, major assets such as aircraft, and even entire factories in finance lease arrangements. The _____ is calculated upon the value of the assets in the same manner as upon money.
a. Interest
b. Interest expense
c. A Mathematical Theory of Communication
d. Interest sensitivity gap

8. In mathematics, a _____ is a number that can be expressed as an integral of an algebraic function over an algebraic domain. Kontsevich and Zagier define a _____ as a complex number whose real and imaginary parts are values of absolutely convergent integrals of rational functions with rational coefficients, over domains in given by polynomial inequalities with rational coefficients.

a. Period
b. Closeness
c. Boussinesq approximation
d. Disk

9. In mathematics, the _____ is an approach to finding a particular solution to certain inhomogeneous ordinary differential equations and recurrence relations. It is closely related to the annihilator method, but instead of using a particular kind of differential operator in order to find the best possible form of the particular solution, a 'guess' is made as to the appropriate form, which is then tested by differentiating the resulting equation. In this sense, the _____ is less formal but more intuitive than the annihilator method.
   a. Linear differential equation
   b. Differential algebraic equations
   c. Phase line
   d. Method of undetermined coefficients

Chapter 12. Compound Interest and Present Value

1. _____ is the concept of adding accumulated interest back to the principal, so that interest is earned on interest from that moment on. The act of declaring interest to be principal is called compounding. A loan, for example, may have its interest compounded every month: in this case, a loan with $100 principal and 1% interest per month would have a balance of $101 at the end of the first month.
    a. Net interest margin
    b. Retained interest
    c. Net interest margin securities
    d. Compound interest

2. _____ is an acronym which stands for last in, first out. In computer science and queueing theory this refers to the way items stored in some types of data structures are processed. By definition, in a _____ structured linear list, elements can be added or taken off from only one end, called the 'top'.
    a. 2-3 heap
    b. LIFO
    c. 1-center problem
    d. 120-cell

3. _____ is a fee, paid on borrowed capital. Assets lent include money, shares, consumer goods through hire purchase, major assets such as aircraft, and even entire factories in finance lease arrangements. The _____ is calculated upon the value of the assets in the same manner as upon money.
    a. Interest sensitivity gap
    b. A Mathematical Theory of Communication
    c. Interest
    d. Interest expense

4. A _____ is the transfer of an interest in property (or in law the equivalent - a charge) to a lender as a security for a debt - usually a loan of money. While a _____ in itself is not a debt, it is lender's security for a debt. It is a transfer of an interest in land (or the equivalent), from the owner to the _____ lender, on the condition that this interest will be returned to the owner of the real estate when the terms of the _____ have been satisfied or performed.
    a. 120-cell
    b. Mortgage
    c. 1-center problem
    d. 2-3 heap

5. In mathematics, a _____ is a number that can be expressed as an integral of an algebraic function over an algebraic domain. Kontsevich and Zagier define a _____ as a complex number whose real and imaginary parts are values of absolutely convergent integrals of rational functions with rational coefficients, over domains in given by polynomial inequalities with rational coefficients.

a. Disk
b. Boussinesq approximation
c. Closeness
d. Period

6. _____ expresses an annual rate of interest taking into account the effect of compounding, usually for deposit or investment products. It is analogous to the Annual percentage rate, which is used for loans. In some jurisdictions, the use and definition of _____ may be regulated by a government agency, in which case it would generally be capitalized.
   a. A Mathematical Theory of Communication
   b. Annual percentage yield
   c. A chemical equation
   d. A posteriori

7. The _____ is the current method of accelerated asset depreciation required by the United States income tax code. Under _____, all assets are divided into classes which dictate the number of years over which an asset's cost will be recovered.

Prior to the Accelerated Cost Recovery System (ACRS), most capital purchases were depreciated using a straight line technique, that allowed for the depreciation of the asset over its useful life.

   a. MACRS
   b. 2-3 heap
   c. 1-center problem
   d. 120-cell

8. In mathematics, a _____ is a way of expressing a number as a fraction of 100. It is often denoted using the percent sign, '%'. For example, 45% is equal to 45 / 100, or 0.45.
   a. Least common multiple
   b. Lowest common denominator
   c. Subtrahend
   d. Percentage

Chapter 13. Annuities and Sinking Funds

1. _____ is an acronym for First In, First Out, an abstraction in ways of organizing and manipulation of data relative to time and prioritization. This expression describes the principle of a queue processing technique or servicing conflicting demands by ordering process by first-come, first-served behaviour: what comes in first is handled first, what comes in next waits until the first is finished, etc.

Thus it is analogous to the behaviour of persons queueing, where the persons leave the queue in the order they arrive, or waiting one's turn at a traffic control signal.

   a. 1-center problem
   b. FIFO
   c. 2-3 heap
   d. 120-cell

Chapter 14. Installment Buying, Rule of 78, and Revolving Charge Credit Cards

1. In mathematics, specifically in combinatorial commutative algebra, a convex lattice polytope P is called _____ if it has the following property: given any positive integer n, every lattice point of the dilation nP, obtained from P by scaling its vertices by the factor n and taking the convex hull of the resulting points, can be written as the sum of exactly n lattice points in P. This property plays an important role in the theory of toric varieties, where it corresponds to projective normality of the toric variety determined by P.

The simplex in R^k with the vertices at the origin and along the unit coordinate vectors is _____.

   a. Demihypercubes
   b. Polytetrahedron
   c. Hypercube
   d. Normal

2. The _____ is an important family of continuous probability distributions, applicable in many fields. Each member of the family may be defined by two parameters, location and scale: the mean and variance respectively. The standard _____ is the _____ with a mean of zero and a variance of one.

   a. Coefficient of variation
   b. Percentile rank
   c. Null hypothesis
   d. Normal distribution

3. In differential geometry, a discipline within mathematics, a _____ is a subset of the tangent bundle of a manifold satisfying certain properties. _____s are used to build up notions of integrability, and specifically of a foliation of a manifold
   a. Discontinuity
   b. Coherence
   c. Constraint
   d. Distribution

4. The terms _____, nominal APR, and effective APR describe the interest rate for a whole year, rather than just a monthly fee/rate, as applied on a loan, mortgage, credit card, etc. Those terms have formal, legal definitions in some countries or legal jurisdictions, but in general:

   - The nominal APR is the simple-interest rate.
   - The effective APR is the fee+compound interest rate.

Chapter 14. Installment Buying, Rule of 78, and Revolving Charge Credit Cards 33

The nominal APR is calculated as: the rate, for a payment period, multiplied by the number of payment periods in a year. However, the exact legal definition of 'effective APR' can vary greatly in each jurisdiction, depending on the type of fees included, such as participation fees, loan origination fees, monthly service charges, or late fees. The effective APR has been called the 'mathematically-true' interest rate for each year. The computation for the effective APR, as the fee+compound interest rate, can also vary depending on whether the up-front fees, such as origination or participation fees, are added to the entire amount, or treated as a short-term loan due in the first payment.

a. A posteriori
b. A Mathematical Theory of Communication
c. A chemical equation
d. Annual percentage rate

5. In mathematics, a _____ is a way of expressing a number as a fraction of 100. It is often denoted using the percent sign, '%'. For example, 45% is equal to 45 / 100, or 0.45.
a. Least common multiple
b. Lowest common denominator
c. Subtrahend
d. Percentage

6. _____ or amortisation is the process of decreasing an amount over a period of time. The word comes from Middle English amortisen to kill, alienate in mortmain, from Anglo-French amorteser, alteration of amortir, from Vulgar Latin admortire to kill, from Latin ad- + mort-, mors death. Particular instances of the term include:

- _____, the allocation of a lump sum amount to different time periods, particularly for loans and other forms of finance, including related interest or other finance charges.
    - _____ schedule, a table detailing each periodic payment on a loan, as generated by an _____ calculator.
    - Negative _____, an _____ schedule where the loan amount actually increases through not paying the full interest
- Amortized analysis, analyzing the execution cost of algorithms over a sequence of operations.
- _____ of capital expenditures of certain assets under accounting rules, particularly intangible assets, in a manner analogous to depreciation.
- _____

_____ is also used in the context of zoning regulations and describes the time in which a property owner has to relocate when the property's use constitutes a preexisting nonconforming use under zoning regulations.

- Depreciation

a. Origin
b. Amortization
c. Identity
d. ISAAC

7. In mathematics, an _____, or central tendency of a data set refers to a measure of the 'middle' or 'expected' value of the data set. There are many different descriptive statistics that can be chosen as a measurement of the central tendency of the data items.

An _____ is a single value that is meant to typify a list of values.

a. A chemical equation
b. A Mathematical Theory of Communication
c. A posteriori
d. Average

Chapter 15. The Cost of Home Ownership

1. _____ is the value of a homeowner's unencumbered interest in their property, i.e. the difference between the home's fair market value and the unpaid balance of the mortgage and any outstanding debt over the home. Equity increases as the mortgage is paid or as the property enjoys appreciation. This is sometimes called real property value in economics.
    a. Real estate
    b. Home equity
    c. 120-cell
    d. 1-center problem

2. A _____ is the transfer of an interest in property (or in law the equivalent - a charge) to a lender as a security for a debt - usually a loan of money. While a _____ in itself is not a debt, it is lender's security for a debt. It is a transfer of an interest in land (or the equivalent), from the owner to the _____ lender, on the condition that this interest will be returned to the owner of the real estate when the terms of the _____ have been satisfied or performed.
    a. 2-3 heap
    b. 120-cell
    c. 1-center problem
    d. Mortgage

3. A _____ is a deliberate process for transforming one or more inputs into one or more results, with variable change.

The term is used in a variety of senses, from the very definite arithmetical using an algorithm to the vague heuristics of calculating a strategy in a competition or calculating the chance of a successful relationship between two people.

Multiplying 7 by 8 is a simple algorithmic _____.

    a. Mathematical object
    b. Mathematics Subject Classification
    c. Calculation
    d. Mathematical maturity

4. _____ is the concept or idea of fairness in economics, particularly as to taxation or welfare economics.
    a. Equity
    b. Union
    c. Interval
    d. Event

Chapter 15. The Cost of Home Ownership

5. In economics, business, retail, and accounting, a _____ is the value of money that has been used up to produce something, and hence is not available for use anymore. In business, the _____ may be one of acquisition, in which case the amount of money expended to acquire it is counted as _____. In this case, money is the input that is gone in order to acquire the thing.
   a. 2-3 heap
   b. Cost
   c. 1-center problem
   d. 120-cell

6. _____ or amortisation is the process of decreasing an amount over a period of time. The word comes from Middle English amortisen to kill, alienate in mortmain, from Anglo-French amorteser, alteration of amortir, from Vulgar Latin admortire to kill, from Latin ad- + mort-, mors death. Particular instances of the term include:

   - _____, the allocation of a lump sum amount to different time periods, particularly for loans and other forms of finance, including related interest or other finance charges.
     o _____ schedule, a table detailing each periodic payment on a loan, as generated by an _____ calculator.
     o Negative _____, an _____ schedule where the loan amount actually increases through not paying the full interest
   - Amortized analysis, analyzing the execution cost of algorithms over a sequence of operations.
   - _____ of capital expenditures of certain assets under accounting rules, particularly intangible assets, in a manner analogous to depreciation.
   - _____

   _____ is also used in the context of zoning regulations and describes the time in which a property owner has to relocate when the property's use constitutes a preexisting nonconforming use under zoning regulations.

   - Depreciation

   a. Identity
   b. Amortization
   c. Origin
   d. ISAAC

7. An _____ is a table detailing each periodic payment on a amortizing loan, as generated by an amortization calculator.

While a portion of every payment is applied towards both the interest and the principal balance of the loan, the exact amount applied to principal each time varies. An _____ reveals the specific monetary amount put towards interest, as well as the specific put towards the Principal balance, with each payment.

a. A chemical equation
b. A Mathematical Theory of Communication
c. Amortization schedule
d. Accounts receivable

Chapter 16. How to Read, Analyze, and Interpret Financial Reports

1. _____ is a file or account that contains money that a person or company owes to suppliers, but hasn't paid yet. When you receive an invoice you add it to the file, and then you remove it when you pay. Thus, the A/P is a form of credit that suppliers offer to their purchasers by allowing them to pay for a product or service after it has already been received.
    a. A Mathematical Theory of Communication
    b. Accounts receivable
    c. A chemical equation
    d. Accounts payable

2. _____ is one of a series of accounting transactions dealing with the billing of customers who owe money to a person, company or organization for goods and services that have been provided to the customer. In most business entities this is typically done by generating an invoice and mailing or electronically delivering it to the customer, who in turn must pay it within an established timeframe called credit or payment terms.

An example of a common payment term is Net 30, meaning payment is due in the amount of the invoice 30 days from the date of invoice.

    a. Accounts receivable
    b. A Mathematical Theory of Communication
    c. Amortization schedule
    d. A chemical equation

3. In financial accounting, a _____ or statement of financial position is a summary of a person's or organization's balances. Assets, liabilities and ownership equity are listed as of a specific date, such as the end of its financial year. A _____ is often described as a snapshot of a company's financial condition.
    a. 1-center problem
    b. 2-3 heap
    c. 120-cell
    d. Balance sheet

4. In mathematics, more particularly in functional analysis, differential topology, and geometric measure theory, a _____ in the sense of Georges de Rham is a functional on the space of compactly supported differential k-forms, on a smooth manifold M. Formally currents behave like Schwartz distributions on a space of differential forms. In a geometric sense they can represent quite singular versions of submanifolds: Dirac delta functions or even multipoles spread out along subsets of M.
    a. Continuous-time Markov process
    b. Convex analysis
    c. Convex and concave
    d. K-current

Chapter 16. How to Read, Analyze, and Interpret Financial Reports

5. _____ is the concept or idea of fairness in economics, particularly as to taxation or welfare economics.
   a. Interval
   b. Equity
   c. Union
   d. Event

6. A _____ is the transfer of an interest in property (or in law the equivalent - a charge) to a lender as a security for a debt - usually a loan of money. While a _____ in itself is not a debt, it is lender's security for a debt. It is a transfer of an interest in land (or the equivalent), from the owner to the _____ lender, on the condition that this interest will be returned to the owner of the real estate when the terms of the _____ have been satisfied or performed.
   a. 2-3 heap
   b. Mortgage
   c. 1-center problem
   d. 120-cell

7. In finance, the Acid-test or _____ or liquid ratio measures the ability of a company to use its near cash or quick assets to immediately extinguish or retire its current liabilities. Quick assets include those current assets that presumably can be quickly converted to cash at close to their book values.

$$\text{Quick (Acid Test) Ratio} = \frac{\text{Cash} + \text{Marketable Securities} + \text{Accounts Receivables}}{\text{Current Liabilities}}$$

Generally, the acid test ratio should be 1:1 or better, however this varies widely by industry.

   a. 1-center problem
   b. 2-3 heap
   c. Quick ratio
   d. 120-cell

8. In economics, _____ is the comparison of two different equilibrium states, before and after a change in some underlying exogenous parameter. As a study of statics it compares two different unchanging points, after they have changed. It does not study the motion towards equilibrium, nor the process of the change itself.
   a. Producer surplus
   b. Marginal rate of technical substitution
   c. Comparative statics
   d. Consumer surplus

9. In economics, business, retail, and accounting, a _____ is the value of money that has been used up to produce something, and hence is not available for use anymore. In business, the _____ may be one of acquisition, in which case the amount of money expended to acquire it is counted as _____. In this case, money is the input that is gone in order to acquire the thing.
a. Cost
b. 2-3 heap
c. 1-center problem
d. 120-cell

10. _____ is defined to be the total invoice value of sales, before deducting customers' discounts, returns, or allowances.

$$\text{Net Sales} = \text{Gross Sales} - (\text{Customer Discounts, Returns, Allowances})$$

a. 1-center problem
b. 120-cell
c. Depreciation
d. Gross sales

11. _____ is a fee, paid on borrowed capital. Assets lent include money, shares, consumer goods through hire purchase, major assets such as aircraft, and even entire factories in finance lease arrangements. The _____ is calculated upon the value of the assets in the same manner as upon money.
a. A Mathematical Theory of Communication
b. Interest expense
c. Interest sensitivity gap
d. Interest

12. _____ is a 2000 epic film directed by Ridley Scott and starring Russell Crowe, Joaquin Phoenix, Connie Nielsen, Oliver Reed, Djimon Hounsou, Derek Jacobi and Richard Harris. Crowe portrays General Maximus Decimus Meridius, friend of Emperor Marcus Aurelius who is betrayed and murdered by his ambitious son, Commodus (Phoenix.) Captured and enslaved along the outer fringes of the Roman empire, Maximus rises through the ranks of the gladiatorial arena to avenge the murder of his family and his Emperor.
a. Agnes Meyer Driscoll
b. Gladiator
c. Adi Shamir
d. Abraham Sinkov

Chapter 16. How to Read, Analyze, and Interpret Financial Reports

13. _____ is one of the principal states of matter. A _____ is a fluid that has the particles loose and can freely form a distinct surface at the boundaries of its bulk material. The surface is a free surface where the _____ is not constrained by a container.
    a. 1-center problem
    b. 120-cell
    c. Liquid
    d. 2-3 heap

14. The term '_____' refers to the concept of collecting information and attempting to spot a pattern in the information. In some fields of study, the term '_____' has more formally-defined meanings.

Although _____ is often used to predict future events, it could be used to estimate uncertain events in the past, such as how many ancient kings probably ruled between two dates, based on data such as the average years which other known kings reigned.

    a. Partial leverage
    b. Probit model
    c. Partial least squares
    d. Trend analysis

15. _____ is a financial ratio that measures the efficiency of a company's use of its assets in generating sales revenue or sales income to the company.

$$Asset\ Turnover = \frac{Sales}{Average Total Assets}$$

- 'Sales' is the value of 'Net Sales' or 'Sales' from the company's income statement
- 'Average Total Assets' is the value of 'Total assets' from the company's balance sheet in the beginning and the end of the fiscal period divided by 2.

- Assets turnover

    a. Asset turnover
    b. A chemical equation
    c. A Mathematical Theory of Communication
    d. A posteriori

Chapter 16. How to Read, Analyze, and Interpret Financial Reports

16. In finance, a _____ or accounting ratio is a ratio of two selected numerical values taken from an enterprise's financial statements. There are many standard ratios used to try to evaluate the overall financial condition of a corporation or other organization. _____s may be used by managers within a firm, by current and potential shareholders (owners) of a firm, and by a firm's creditors.
    a. Financial ratio
    b. Return on equity
    c. P/E ratio
    d. 1-center problem

17. _____ measures the rate of return on the ownership interest (shareholders' equity) of the common stock owners. _____ is viewed as one of the most important financial ratios. It measures a firm's efficiency at generating profits from every dollar of net assets (assets minus liabilities), and shows how well a company uses investment dollars to generate earnings growth.
    a. Rate of return
    b. 1-center problem
    c. Return on equity
    d. P/E ratio

Chapter 17. Depreciation

1. In accounting, _____ or carrying value is the value of an asset or according to its balance sheet account balance. For assets, the value is based on the original cost of the asset less any depreciation, amortization or impairment costs made against the asset. A company's _____ is its total assets minus intangible assets and liabilities.
    a. 1-center problem
    b. Depreciation
    c. 120-cell
    d. Book value

2. _____ is a term used in accounting, economics and finance to spread the cost of an asset over the span of several years.

In simple words we can say that _____ is the reduction in the value of an asset due to usage, passage of time, wear and tear, technological outdating or obsolescence, depletion or other such factors.

In accounting, _____ is a term used to describe any method of attributing the historical or purchase cost of an asset across its useful life, roughly corresponding to normal wear and tear.

    a. Gross sales
    b. 120-cell
    c. 1-center problem
    d. Depreciation

3. _____ refers to any one of several methods by which a company, for 'financial accounting' and/or tax purposes, depreciates a fixed asset in such a way that the amount of depreciation taken each year is higher during the earlier years of an asset's life. For financial accounting purposes, _____ is generally used when an asset is expected to be much more productive during its early years, so that depreciation expense will more accurately represent how much of an asset's usefulness is being used up each year. For tax purposes, _____ provides a way of deferring corporate income taxes by reducing taxable income in current years, in exchange for increased taxable income in future years.
    a. A posteriori
    b. A Mathematical Theory of Communication
    c. A chemical equation
    d. Accelerated depreciation

4. _____ is a fee, paid on borrowed capital. Assets lent include money, shares, consumer goods through hire purchase, major assets such as aircraft, and even entire factories in finance lease arrangements. The _____ is calculated upon the value of the assets in the same manner as upon money.

a. Interest expense
b. Interest sensitivity gap
c. A Mathematical Theory of Communication
d. Interest

5. In abstract algebra, a module S over a ring R is called _____ or irreducible if it is not the zero module 0 and if its only submodules are 0 and S. Understanding the _____ modules over a ring is usually helpful because these modules form the 'building blocks' of all other modules in a certain sense.

Abelian groups are the same as Z-modules.

a. Harmonic series
b. Basis
c. Derivation
d. Simple

Chapter 18. Inventory and Overhead

1. _____ is an acronym which stands for last in, first out. In computer science and queueing theory this refers to the way items stored in some types of data structures are processed. By definition, in a _____ structured linear list, elements can be added or taken off from only one end, called the 'top'.

   a. 120-cell
   b. 1-center problem
   c. 2-3 heap
   d. LIFO

2. _____ is an acronym for First In, First Out, an abstraction in ways of organizing and manipulation of data relative to time and prioritization. This expression describes the principle of a queue processing technique or servicing conflicting demands by ordering process by first-come, first-served behaviour: what comes in first is handled first, what comes in next waits until the first is finished, etc.

   Thus it is analogous to the behaviour of persons queueing, where the persons leave the queue in the order they arrive, or waiting one's turn at a traffic control signal.

   a. FIFO
   b. 2-3 heap
   c. 120-cell
   d. 1-center problem

3. In accounting, _____ or sales profit is the difference between revenue and the cost of making a product or providing a service, before deducting overhead, payroll, taxation, and interest payments. Note that this is different than operating profit.

Net sales are calculated:

    Net sales = Sales - Sales returns and allowances

_____ is found by deducting the cost of goods sold:

    _____ = Net sales - Cost of goods sold

_____ should not be confused with net income:

    Net income = _____ - Total operating expenses

Cost of goods sold is calculated differently for merchandising business than for a manufacturer.

a. Gross profit
b. 2-3 heap
c. 120-cell
d. 1-center problem

4. In mathematics, an _____, or central tendency of a data set refers to a measure of the 'middle' or 'expected' value of the data set. There are many different descriptive statistics that can be chosen as a measurement of the central tendency of the data items.

An _____ is a single value that is meant to typify a list of values.

a. A Mathematical Theory of Communication
b. A posteriori
c. Average
d. A chemical equation

5. In differential geometry, a discipline within mathematics, a _____ is a subset of the tangent bundle of a manifold satisfying certain properties. _____s are used to build up notions of integrability, and specifically of a foliation of a manifold
a. Discontinuity
b. Coherence
c. Constraint
d. Distribution

Chapter 19. Sales, Excise, and Property Taxes

1. A vulgar fraction (or common fraction) is a rational number written as one integer (the numerator) divided by a non-zero integer (the denominator).

A vulgar fraction is said to be a _____ if the absolute value of the numerator is less than the absolute value of the denominator--that is, if the absolute value of the entire fraction is less than 1.

   a. Proper fraction
   b. 120-cell
   c. Farey sequence
   d. 1-center problem

2. The _____ is the current method of accelerated asset depreciation required by the United States income tax code. Under _____, all assets are divided into classes which dictate the number of years over which an asset's cost will be recovered.

Prior to the Accelerated Cost Recovery System (ACRS), most capital purchases were depreciated using a straight line technique, that allowed for the depreciation of the asset over its useful life.

   a. 1-center problem
   b. 2-3 heap
   c. MACRS
   d. 120-cell

Chapter 20. Life, Fire, and Auto Insurance

1. The term _____ refers to the central sense organ complex, for those animals that have one, normally on the ventral surface of the head and can depending on the definition in the human case, include the hair, forehead, eyebrow, eyes, nose, ears, cheeks, mouth, lips, philtrum, teeth, skin, and chin. The _____ has uses of expression, appearance, and identity amongst others.It also has different senses like smelling, tasting, hearing, and seeing.

Caricatures often exaggerate facial features to make a _____ more easily recognized in association with a pronounced portion of the _____ of the individual in question--for example, a caricature of Osama bin Laden might focus on his facial hair and nose; a caricature of George W. Bush might enlarge his ears to the size of an elephant¢s; a caricature of Jay Leno may pronounce his head and chin; and a caricature of Mick Jagger might enlarge his lips.

   a. 120-cell
   b. 2-3 heap
   c. 1-center problem
   d. Face

2. _____ is the mathematical operation of scaling one number by another. It is one of the four basic operations in elementary arithmetic.

_____ is defined for whole numbers in terms of repeated addition; for example, 4 multiplied by 3 can be calculated by adding 3 copies of 4 together:

$$4 + 4 + 4 = 12.$$

_____ of rational numbers and real numbers is defined by systematic generalization of this basic idea.

   a. Highest common factor
   b. Multiplication
   c. Least common multiple
   d. The number 0 is even.

3. _____ is the concept of adding accumulated interest back to the principal, so that interest is earned on interest from that moment on. The act of declaring interest to be principal is called compounding. A loan, for example, may have its interest compounded every month: in this case, a loan with $100 principal and 1% interest per month would have a balance of $101 at the end of the first month.
   a. Net interest margin securities
   b. Net interest margin
   c. Compound interest
   d. Retained interest

Chapter 20. Life, Fire, and Auto Insurance

4. _____ is a fee, paid on borrowed capital. Assets lent include money, shares, consumer goods through hire purchase, major assets such as aircraft, and even entire factories in finance lease arrangements. The _____ is calculated upon the value of the assets in the same manner as upon money.

   a. Interest
   b. Interest expense
   c. A Mathematical Theory of Communication
   d. Interest sensitivity gap

5. A _____ is a deliberate plan of action to guide decisions and achieve rational outcom. The term may apply to government, private sector organizations and groups, and individuals. Presidential executive orders, corporate privacy policies, and parliamentary rules of order are all examples of _____.

   a. 120-cell
   b. 1-center problem
   c. 2-3 heap
   d. Policy

6. The _____ of an insurance contract is the cash amount offered to the policyowner by the issuing life carrier upon cancellation of the contract. This term is normally used with a life insurance contract.

To receive the _____, the policyholder is normally obliged to surrender the policy received at outset of the contract to the issuing life insurance company as documentation of rights under the contract.

   a. 1-center problem
   b. Cash value
   c. 2-3 heap
   d. 120-cell

7. In a graph theory, the _____ L

One of the earliest and most important theorems about _____s is due to Hassler Whitney, who proved that with one exceptional case the structure of G can be recovered completely from its _____.

   a. Vertex-transitive graph
   b. Bivariegated graph
   c. Sparse graph
   d. Line graph

Chapter 20. Life, Fire, and Auto Insurance

8. In Fourier analysis, a _____ is a kind of linear operator, or transformation of functions. These operators multiply the Fourier coefficients of a function by a specified function, hence the name. Among the multipliers one can count some simple operators, such as translations and differentiation, but also some more complicated ones such as the convolutions, Hilbert transform, and others.
   a. Fourier multiplier
   b. Poisson summation formula
   c. Reality condition
   d. Modulated complex lapped transform

9. In mathematics, especially in the field of ring theory, a (left) _____ is a ring in which all left ideals are free of unique rank. A ring such that all left ideals with at most n generators is free of unique rank is called an n-fir. A semi-fir is a ring in which all finitely generated left ideals are free of unique rank.
   a. Free ideal ring
   b. Group ring
   c. Product ring
   d. Noetherian ring

10. In mathematics, a _____ of a set X is a collection of sets such that X is a subset of the union of sets in the collection. In symbols, if

$$C = \{U_\alpha : \alpha \in A\}$$

is an indexed family of sets U_α, then C is a _____ of X if

$$X \subseteq \bigcup_{\alpha \in A} U_\alpha$$

_____s are commonly used in the context of topology. If the set X is a topological space, then a _____ C of X is a collection of subsets U_α of X whose union is the whole space X.

   a. Contractible space
   b. Manifold
   c. Generalised metric
   d. Cover

11. A _____ is an isolated event in which two or more bodies exert relatively strong forces on each other for a relatively short time. Deflection happens when an object hits a plane surface

_____s involve forces. _____s can be elastic, meaning they conserve energy and momentum, inelastic, meaning they conserve momentum but not energy, or totally inelastic, meaning they conserve momentum and the two objects stick together.

a. Parallel axes rule
b. 1-center problem
c. 120-cell
d. Collision

Chapter 21. Stocks, Bonds, and Mutual Funds

1. A _____ is an official document affirming some fact. For example, a birth _____ or death _____ testifies to basic facts regarding a person's birth or death. A _____ may also certify that a person has received specific education or has passed a test, and is considered below the standard of an academic degree.

    a. 120-cell
    b. 1-center problem
    c. 2-3 heap
    d. Certificate

2. A _____ is a party that mediates between a buyer and a seller. A _____ who also acts as a seller or as a buyer becomes a principal party to the deal. Distinguish agent: one who acts on behalf of a principal.

    a. 120-cell
    b. 2-3 heap
    c. 1-center problem
    d. Broker

3. _____s are payments made by a corporation to its shareholder members. When a corporation earns a profit or surplus, that money can be put to two uses: it can either be re-invested in the business, or it can be paid to the shareholders as a _____. Many corporations retain a portion of their earnings and pay the remainder as a _____.

    a. 120-cell
    b. 1-center problem
    c. GNU Privacy Guard
    d. Dividend

4. In mathematics, more particularly in functional analysis, differential topology, and geometric measure theory, a _____ in the sense of Georges de Rham is a functional on the space of compactly supported differential k-forms, on a smooth manifold M. Formally currents behave like Schwartz distributions on a space of differential forms. In a geometric sense they can represent quite singular versions of submanifolds: Dirac delta functions or even multipoles spread out along subsets of M.

    a. Continuous-time Markov process
    b. Convex analysis
    c. Convex and concave
    d. K-current

5. In economics, business, retail, and accounting, a _____ is the value of money that has been used up to produce something, and hence is not available for use anymore. In business, the _____ may be one of acquisition, in which case the amount of money expended to acquire it is counted as _____. In this case, money is the input that is gone in order to acquire the thing.
   a. 2-3 heap
   b. 120-cell
   c. 1-center problem
   d. Cost

Chapter 22. Business Statistics

1. In mathematics, an _____, or central tendency of a data set refers to a measure of the 'middle' or 'expected' value of the data set. There are many different descriptive statistics that can be chosen as a measurement of the central tendency of the data items.

An _____ is a single value that is meant to typify a list of values.

   a. A chemical equation
   b. A posteriori
   c. A Mathematical Theory of Communication
   d. Average

2. In statistics, _____ has two related meanings:

   - the arithmetic _____.
   - the expected value of a random variable, which is also called the population _____.

It is sometimes stated that the '_____' _____s average. This is incorrect if '_____' is taken in the specific sense of 'arithmetic _____' as there are different types of averages: the _____, median, and mode. For instance, average house prices almost always use the median value for the average.

For a real-valued random variable X, the _____ is the expectation of X.

   a. Proportional hazards model
   b. Mean
   c. Probability
   d. Statistical population

3. In statistics, the _____ is the value that occurs the most frequently in a data set or a probability distribution. In some fields, notably education, sample data are often called scores, and the sample _____ is known as the modal score.

Like the statistical mean and the median, the _____ is a way of capturing important information about a random variable or a population in a single quantity.

   a. Deltoid
   b. Function
   c. Field
   d. Mode

4. The _____ is similar to an arithmetic mean, where instead of each of the data points contributing equally to the final average, some data points contribute more than others. The notion of _____ plays a role in descriptive statistics and also occurs in a more general form in several other areas of mathematics.

If all the weights are equal, then the _____ is the same as the arithmetic mean.

   a. Quasi-arithmetic mean
   b. Truncated mean
   c. Mid-range
   d. Weighted mean

5. A _____ is a deliberate process for transforming one or more inputs into one or more results, with variable change.

The term is used in a variety of senses, from the very definite arithmetical using an algorithm to the vague heuristics of calculating a strategy in a competition or calculating the chance of a successful relationship between two people.

Multiplying 7 by 8 is a simple algorithmic _____.

   a. Mathematical object
   b. Mathematics Subject Classification
   c. Mathematical maturity
   d. Calculation

6. In geometry, a _____ of a triangle is a line segment joining a vertex to the midpoint of the opposing side. Every triangle has exactly three _____s; one running from each vertex to the opposite side.

The three _____s are concurrent at a point known as the triangle's centroid, or center of mass of the triangle.

   a. Statistical significance
   b. Correlation
   c. Median
   d. Percentile rank

7. In statistics the _____ of an event i is the number n_i of times the event occurred in the experiment or the study. These frequencies are often graphically represented in histograms.

We speak of absolute frequencies, when the counts n_i themselves are given and of

$$f_i = \frac{n_i}{N} = \frac{n_i}{\sum_i n_i}$$

Taking the f_i for all i and tabulating or plotting them leads to a _____ distribution.

   a. Subharmonic
   b. Digital room correction
   c. Robinson-Dadson curves
   d. Frequency

8. In statistics, a _____ is a list of the values that a variable takes in a sample. It is usually a list, ordered by quantity, showing the number of times each value appears. For example, if 100 people rate a five-point Likert scale assessing their agreement with a statement on a scale on which 1 denotes strong agreement and 5 strong disagreement, the _____ of their responses might look like:

This simple tabulation has two drawbacks.

   a. Percentile
   b. Confounding
   c. Frequency distribution
   d. Covariance

9. In differential geometry, a discipline within mathematics, a _____ is a subset of the tangent bundle of a manifold satisfying certain properties. _____s are used to build up notions of integrability, and specifically of a foliation of a manifold
   a. Discontinuity
   b. Constraint
   c. Coherence
   d. Distribution

10. A bar chart or _____ is a chart with rectangular bars with lengths proportional to the values that they represent. Bar charts are used for comparing two or more values. The bars can be horizontally or vertically oriented.

a. 120-cell
b. 1-center problem
c. 2-3 heap
d. Bar graph

11. A _____ is a simple shape of Euclidean geometry consisting of those points in a plane which are at a constant distance, called the radius, from a fixed point, called the center. A _____ with center A is sometimes denoted by the symbol A.

A chord of a _____ is a line segment whose two endpoints lie on the _____.

a. Circular segment
b. Malfatti circles
c. Circumcircle
d. Circle

12. In graph theory, a _____ is a graph whose vertices can be associated with chords of a circle such that two vertices are adjacent if and only if the corresponding chords in the circle intersect.

Spinrad (1994) gives an $O(n^2)$-time recognition algorithm for _____s that also computes a circle model of the input graph if it is a _____.

A number of other problems that are NP-complete on general graphs have polynomial time algorithms when restricted to _____s.

a. Vertex-transitive graph
b. Circle graph
c. Sparse graph
d. Planar graph

13. In a graph theory, the _____ L

One of the earliest and most important theorems about _____s is due to Hassler Whitney, who proved that with one exceptional case the structure of G can be recovered completely from its _____.

a. Vertex-transitive graph
b. Sparse graph
c. Bivariegated graph
d. Line graph

14. In mathematics the concept of a _____ generalizes notions such as 'length', 'area', and 'volume'. Informally, given some base set, a '_____' is any consistent assignment of 'sizes' to the subsets of the base set. Depending on the application, the 'size' of a subset may be interpreted as its physical size, the amount of something that lies within the subset, or the probability that some random process will yield a result within the subset.
   a. Congruent
   b. Cusp
   c. Lattice
   d. Measure

15. In optics, _____ is the phenomenon in which the phase velocity of a wave depends on its frequency. Media having such a property are termed dispersive media.

The most familiar example of _____ is probably a rainbow, in which _____ causes the spatial separation of a white light into components of different wavelengths.

   a. Depth
   b. Crib
   c. Boussinesq approximation
   d. Dispersion

16. In probability and statistics, the _____ is a measure of the dispersion of a collection of numbers. It can apply to a probability distribution, a random variable, a population or a data set. The _____ is usually denoted with the letter σ.
   a. Null hypothesis
   b. Statistical population
   c. Failure rate
   d. Standard deviation

17. In mathematics and statistics, _____ is a measure of difference for interval and ratio variables between the observed value and the mean. The sign of _____, either positive or negative, indicates whether the observation is larger than or smaller than the mean. The magnitude of the value reports how different an observation is from the mean.

a. Conchoid
b. Functional
c. Deviation
d. Filter

18. In mathematics, specifically in combinatorial commutative algebra, a convex lattice polytope P is called _____ if it has the following property: given any positive integer n, every lattice point of the dilation nP, obtained from P by scaling its vertices by the factor n and taking the convex hull of the resulting points, can be written as the sum of exactly n lattice points in P. This property plays an important role in the theory of toric varieties, where it corresponds to projective normality of the toric variety determined by P.

The simplex in R^k with the vertices at the origin and along the unit coordinate vectors is _____.

a. Hypercube
b. Normal
c. Polytetrahedron
d. Demihypercubes

19. The _____ is an important family of continuous probability distributions, applicable in many fields. Each member of the family may be defined by two parameters, location and scale: the mean and variance respectively. The standard _____ is the _____ with a mean of zero and a variance of one.

a. Null hypothesis
b. Coefficient of variation
c. Percentile rank
d. Normal distribution

20. In descriptive statistics, the _____ is the length of the smallest interval which contains all the data. It is calculated by subtracting the smallest observations from the greatest and provides an indication of statistical dispersion.

It is measured in the same units as the data.

a. Class
b. Kernel
c. Bandwidth
d. Range

ANSWER KEY

Chapter 1
    1. c   2. c   3. a   4. d   5. c   6. d   7. d   8. a   9. b   10. d
    11. c   12. d   13. c   14. d   15. b   16. d   17. b   18. d

Chapter 2
    1. a   2. d   3. b   4. d   5. c   6. c   7. c   8. a   9. a   10. d

Chapter 3
    1. b   2. a   3. d   4. c   5. a

Chapter 4
    1. d   2. d   3. b

Chapter 5
    1. b   2. d

Chapter 6
    1. d   2. a   3. a   4. c   5. c   6. b

Chapter 7
    1. b   2. b   3. c   4. d   5. c   6. c   7. d   8. b   9. d   10. b
    11. a   12. b

Chapter 8
    1. b   2. b   3. b   4. d   5. a

Chapter 9
    1. b   2. d   3. d   4. c   5. a   6. d   7. b

Chapter 10
    1. d   2. d   3. d   4. d   5. d

Chapter 11
    1. d   2. d   3. b   4. d   5. d   6. c   7. a   8. a   9. d

Chapter 12
    1. d   2. b   3. c   4. b   5. d   6. b   7. a   8. d

Chapter 13
    1. b

Chapter 14
    1. d   2. d   3. d   4. d   5. d   6. b   7. d

ANSWER KEY

Chapter 15
1. b   2. d   3. c   4. a   5. b   6. b   7. c

Chapter 16
1. d   2. a   3. d   4. d   5. b   6. b   7. c   8. c   9. a   10. d
11. d   12. b   13. c   14. d   15. a   16. a   17. c

Chapter 17
1. d   2. d   3. d   4. d   5. d

Chapter 18
1. d   2. a   3. a   4. c   5. d

Chapter 19
1. a   2. c

Chapter 20
1. d   2. b   3. c   4. a   5. d   6. b   7. d   8. a   9. a   10. d
11. d

Chapter 21
1. d   2. d   3. d   4. d   5. d

Chapter 22
1. d   2. b   3. d   4. d   5. d   6. c   7. d   8. c   9. d   10. d
11. d   12. b   13. d   14. d   15. d   16. d   17. c   18. b   19. d   20. d

www.ingramcontent.com/pod-product-compliance
Lightning Source LLC
Chambersburg PA
CBHW081219230426
43666CB00015B/2803